Country Cookin'
Sunday Suppers

pil

Publications International, Ltd.
www.pilcookbooks.com

Pictured on the front cover: Southern Fried Catfish with Hush Puppies *(page 52).*
Pictured on the back cover *(left to right):* Harvest Fruit Stuffing *(page 68)* and Apple Pecan Cheesecake *(page 86).*

ISBN-13: 978-1-60553-258-5
ISBN-10: 1-60553-258-4

Manufactured in China.

8 7 6 5 4 3 2 1

Microwave Cooking: Microwave ovens vary in wattage. Use the cooking times as guidelines and check for doneness before adding more time.

Preparation/Cooking Times: Preparation times are based on the approximate amount of time required to assemble the recipe before cooking, baking, chilling or serving. These times include preparation steps such as measuring, chopping and mixing. The fact that some preparations and cooking can be done simultaneously is taken into account. Preparation of optional ingredients and serving suggestions is not included.

pil

Publications International, Ltd.
www.pilcookbooks.com

Contents

Chicken and Three-Pepper Corn Chowder

12 *Tyson®* Individually Frozen Boneless Skinless Chicken Tenderloins, thawed, cut into bite-size pieces

2 tablespoons butter or margarine

3 cups frozen pepper and onion stir-fry mixture

1 large clove garlic, minced

2 cups frozen corn

1 cup chicken broth

1/8 teaspoon ground red pepper

2 cups (8 ounces) shredded or diced pasteurized process cheese product

1/2 cup whipping cream

1 tablespoon chopped fresh cilantro

4 cilantro sprigs (optional)

1. Wash hands. In large skillet, melt butter over medium heat. Add frozen vegetables; cook and stir 5 to 7 minutes or until tender. Add garlic; stir 30 seconds. Remove vegetables and set aside.

2. Add chicken tenders, corn, broth and red pepper to skillet; bring to a boil. Reduce heat; cover and simmer 5 minutes. Over medium heat, add cheese and cream to chicken mixture. Cook and stir until cheese is melted and internal juices of chicken run clear. (Or insert instant-read meat thermometer into thickest part of chicken. Temperature should read 180°F.) Stir in chopped cilantro.

3. Ladle into individual bowls. Garnish with cilantro sprigs. Refrigerate leftovers immediately.   *Makes 4 servings*

Cook Time: 25 minutes

Idaho Potato Chili

1 pound Idaho Potatoes, peeled and cut into ½-inch cubes
   (about 2½ cups)
1 tablespoon vegetable oil
1 large onion, chopped (about 1 cup)
1 green bell pepper, diced (about 1 cup)
1 clove garlic, minced
8 ounces ground turkey
2 tablespoons chili powder
1 can (28 ounces) whole tomatoes, undrained
1 can (16 ounces) kidney beans, drained and rinsed
1 cup water
½ teaspoon salt
¼ cup chopped fresh cilantro
¼ cup plain nonfat yogurt or 2 tablespoons low-fat sour cream
¼ cup sliced green onions or chopped tomato (optional)

1. Heat oil in large saucepan over medium-high heat. Add onion, pepper and garlic. Cook and stir 5 minutes or until softened.

2. Add turkey. Cook and stir 5 to 6 minutes or until no longer pink, breaking up with spoon.

3. Stir in chili powder. Cook for 1 minute. Add canned tomatoes with juice, potatoes, beans, water and salt. Bring to a boil. Reduce heat to low. Simmer, covered, 30 minutes, stirring occasionally.

4. Remove from heat. Stir in cilantro. Top with yogurt and green onions, if desired.
Makes 4 to 6 servings

Favorite recipe from **Idaho Potato Commission**

Idaho Potato Chili

Hearty Beef and Bean Chili

2½ pounds boneless chuck roast, cut into large chunks
1 can (28 ounces) HUNT'S® Whole Peeled Tomatoes
1 can (6 ounces) HUNT'S® Tomato Paste
1 can (30 ounces) HUNT'S® Chili Beans
1 package (1.25 ounces) chili seasoning mix

Slow Cooker Directions

Combine roast, tomatoes, tomato paste, beans and seasoning mix in slow cooker.

Cover; cook on LOW for 8 to 10 hours or on HIGH for 4 to 6 hours until meat is
tender. *Makes 8 servings (1 cup each)*

Hands On: 5 minutes
Total Time: 8 to 10 hours (LOW) or 4 to 6 hours (HIGH)

Bacon-Ham Chowder

1 cup radiatore or other small shaped pasta
½ pound sliced bacon
4 chicken bouillon cubes
2 cups water
5 small potatoes, cubed (about 5 cups)
1 bunch green onions, chopped
1 cup sliced carrots
4 cups whole milk
½ cup all-purpose flour
1½ cups cubed cooked ham
1 tablespoon hot pepper sauce
Cracked black pepper, to taste
1 cup shredded Cheddar cheese

Cook pasta according to package directions until tender but firm; do not overcook.

Cook bacon until crisp and set aside. When cool, crumble into bite-size pieces.
Combine bouillon and water in large pan; heat to boiling. Add potatoes; cover and
simmer 5 minutes.

Add onions and carrots and simmer until vegetables are tender, about 10 to
12 minutes. Whisk milk and flour together; add to vegetables. Cook over medium

heat, stirring frequently until bubbly and thickened. Add ham, bacon, pepper sauce, cracked pepper, pasta and cheese and heat until cheese is melted.

Makes 6 servings

Favorite recipe from **North Dakota Wheat Commission**

Hearty Chicken Chili

1 medium onion, finely chopped

1 small jalapeño pepper,* minced

1 clove garlic, minced

1½ teaspoons chili powder

¾ teaspoon salt

½ teaspoon ground cumin

½ teaspoon dried oregano

½ teaspoon black pepper

¼ teaspoon red pepper flakes (optional)

1½ pounds boneless skinless chicken thighs, cut into 1-inch pieces

2 cans (about 15 ounces each) hominy, rinsed and drained

1 can (about 15 ounces) pinto beans, rinsed and drained

1 cup chicken broth

1 tablespoon all-purpose flour (optional)

Chopped fresh parsley or fresh cilantro (optional)

*Jalapeño peppers can sting and irritate the skin, so wear rubber gloves when handling peppers and do not touch your eyes.

Slow Cooker Directions

1. Combine onion, jalapeño, garlic, chili powder, salt, cumin, oregano, black pepper and pepper flakes, if desired, in slow cooker.

2. Add chicken, hominy, beans and broth. Stir well to combine. Cover; cook on LOW 7 hours.

3. If thicker gravy is desired, combine 1 tablespoon flour and 3 tablespoons cooking liquid in small bowl. Add to slow cooker. Cover; cook on HIGH 10 minutes or until thickened. Serve in bowls and garnish with parsley.

Makes 6 servings

Prep Time: 15 minutes
Cook Time: 7 hours (LOW), plus 10 minutes (HIGH)

Corn and Buttermilk
Blender Chowder

   3 cups cold buttermilk, divided
   2 cups corn
   3 green onions, coarsely chopped
1½ tablespoons coarsely chopped fresh cilantro, plus additional for
      garnish
   ¼ teaspoon salt
   ⅛ teaspoon black pepper

1. Combine 1 cup buttermilk, corn, green onions, cilantro, salt and pepper in blender. Pulse until corn and green onions are minced. Pour mixture into pitcher with remaining 2 cups buttermilk.

2. Serve immediately or refrigerate up to 4 hours. Stir well before serving. Garnish with additional cilantro. *Makes 4 servings*

Head-'Em-Off-at-the-Pass
White Chili

   1 tablespoon olive oil
   ½ cup chopped onion
   2 cans (15 ounces each) cannellini beans, undrained
   1 jar (11 ounces) NEWMAN'S OWN® Bandito Salsa, divided
1½ cups chopped cooked chicken
   ½ cup chicken broth
   1 teaspoon oregano leaves
   ½ teaspoon celery salt
1½ cups (6 ounces) shredded mozzarella cheese, divided

Heat oil in 2-quart saucepan; add onion and cook and stir until tender. Stir in beans, ½ cup of Newman's Own® Bandito Salsa, chicken, chicken broth, oregano and celery salt. Cover; simmer over medium heat 10 minutes, stirring occasionally. Just before serving, stir in 1 cup of mozzarella cheese. Divide chili evenly among serving bowls. Top each with a portion of remaining mozzarella and salsa. *Makes 4 servings*

Corn and Buttermilk Blender Chowder

Hearty Corn Chowder

PAM® Original No-Stick Cooking Spray
1 package (46 ounces) frozen Banquet® Crock-Pot Classics® Chicken
with Red Skin Potatoes and Vegetables
1¾ cups vegetable stock
1 bag (16 ounces) frozen corn
1 can (12 ounces) evaporated milk
½ cup cooked, chopped bacon (about 12 slices), divided

Slow Cooker Directions

1. Spray insert of 4-quart CROCK-POT® slow cooker with cooking spray.

2. Prepare CROCK-POT® meal sauce pouch according to package directions. Place potato pouch on plate in refrigerator. Pour sauce into slow cooker; add vegetable stock (omit water) and stir until dissolved.

3. Stir in chicken and vegetables from package plus corn. Cover and cook on LOW 8 to 10 hours or on HIGH 4 hours.

4. Add refrigerated potatoes and evaporated milk 35 minutes prior to serving. Stir to blend; cover and cook remaining 35 minutes.

5. Serve immediately, garnishing each serving with 1 tablespoon chopped bacon.

Makes 8 servings (1 cup each)

Keep the lid on!
Slow cookers can take up
to 30 minutes to regain
heat lost when the cover is
removed. Only remove the
cover when instructed to do
so by the recipe.

Hearty Corn Chowder

Smokin' Texas Chili

2 tablespoons olive oil

1½ pounds boneless beef sirloin steak or top round steak, ¾-inch thick, cut into ½-inch pieces

1 medium onion, chopped (about ½ cup)

2 cloves garlic, minced

3 cups PACE® Chunky Salsa, any variety

½ cup water

1 tablespoon chili powder

1 teaspoon ground cumin

1 can (about 15 ounces) red kidney beans, rinsed and drained

¼ cup chopped fresh cilantro leaves

Chili Toppings (optional)

1. Heat 1 tablespoon oil in a 6-quart saucepot over medium-high heat. Add the beef in 2 batches and cook until it's well browned, stirring often. Remove the beef from the saucepot.

2. Add the remaining oil and heat over medium heat. Add the onion and cook until it's tender. Add the garlic and cook for 30 seconds.

3. Add the salsa, water, chili powder and cumin. Heat to a boil. Return the beef to the saucepot. Stir in the beans. Reduce the heat to low. Cover and cook for 1 hour. Uncover and cook for 30 minutes or until the beef is fork-tender.

4. Sprinkle with the cilantro and Chili Toppings, if desired.   *Makes 6 servings*

Chili Toppings: Chopped tomatoes, chopped onions, sour cream or shredded cheese.

Prep Time: 15 minutes
Cook Time: 1 hour, 45 minutes

Smokin' Texas Chili

Double Corn Chowder

    1 cup corn

    1 cup canned hominy

    6 ounces Canadian bacon, chopped

    2 stalks celery, chopped

    1 small onion or 1 large shallot, chopped

    1 jalapeño pepper,* seeded and minced

    ¼ teaspoon salt

    ¼ teaspoon dried thyme

    ¼ teaspoon black pepper

    1 cup chicken broth

 1½ cups milk,** divided

    1 tablespoon all-purpose flour

*Jalapeño peppers can sting and irritate the skin, so wear rubber gloves when handling peppers and do not touch your eyes.

**For richer chowder, use ¾ cup milk and ¾ cup half-and-half.

Slow Cooker Directions

1. Combine corn, hominy, bacon, celery, onion, jalapeño, salt, thyme and black pepper in 4-quart slow cooker. Add broth. Cover; cook on LOW 5 to 6 hours or on HIGH 3 to 3½ hours.

2. Whisk 2 tablespoons milk and flour in small bowl. Stir into corn mixture. Add remaining milk. Cover; cook on LOW 20 minutes or until slightly thickened and heated through.

Makes 4 servings

Double Corn Chowder

Super Chili for a Crowd

2 large onions, chopped
1 tablespoon minced garlic
2 pounds boneless top round or sirloin steak, cut into ½-inch cubes
1 pound ground beef
1 can (28 ounces) crushed tomatoes in purée
1 can (15 to 19 ounces) red kidney beans, undrained
⅓ cup *Frank's® RedHot®* Original Cayenne Pepper Sauce
2 packages (1¼ ounces each) chili seasoning mix

1. Heat 1 tablespoon oil in 5-quart saucepot or Dutch oven until hot. Sauté onions and garlic until tender; transfer to bowl.

2. Heat 3 tablespoons oil in same pot; cook meat in batches until well browned. Drain fat.

3. Add ¾ cup water and remaining ingredients to pot. Stir in onion and garlic. Heat to boiling, stirring. Simmer, partially covered, for 1 hour or until meat is tender, stirring often. Garnish as desired.   *Makes 10 servings*

Prep Time: 15 minutes
Cook Time: 1 hour 15 minutes

Best Ever Chili

1½ pounds ground beef
1 cup chopped onion
2 cans (about 15 ounces each) kidney beans, 1 cup juice reserved
1½ pounds plum tomatoes, diced
1 can (about 15 ounces) tomato paste
3 to 6 tablespoons chili powder

Slow Cooker Directions

1. Cook and stir beef and onion in large skillet over medium-high heat, stirring to break up meat, 10 minutes or until no longer pink. Drain; transfer to slow cooker.

2. Add kidney beans, tomatoes, tomato paste, reserved bean juice and chili powder to slow cooker; mix well. Cover; cook on LOW 10 to 12 hours.

Makes 8 servings

Super Chili for a Crowd

Country Chicken Chowder

   2 tablespoons butter or margarine
1½ pounds chicken tenders, cut into ½-inch pieces
   2 small onions, chopped
   2 stalks celery, sliced
   2 small carrots, sliced
   2 cups frozen corn
   2 cans (10¾ ounces each) cream of potato soup
1½ cups chicken broth
   1 teaspoon dried dill weed
   ½ cup half-and-half

Slow Cooker Directions

1. Melt butter in large skillet. Add chicken; cook until browned. Transfer to slow cooker. Top with onions, celery, carrots, corn, soup, broth and dill. Cover; cook on LOW 3 to 4 hours.

2. Turn off heat; stir in half-and-half. Cover and let stand 5 to 10 minutes or until heated through.
Makes 8 servings

Creamy Roasted Garlic & Potato Chowder

   2 cups 1% milk
1½ cups water
   1 tablespoon HERB-OX® chicken flavored bouillon
   1 cup refrigerated diced potatoes
   ½ cup frozen whole kernel corn, thawed
   ¼ cup light roasted garlic flavored cream cheese
1¼ cups instant mashed potato flakes
   ¼ cup finely shredded Cheddar cheese
   ¼ cup sliced green onions
   ¼ cup crumbled HORMEL® fully cooked bacon or
       HORMEL® real bacon bits

In saucepan, bring milk, water, bouillon and refrigerated potatoes to a boil. Reduce heat and simmer for 5 to 8 minutes or until potatoes are tender. Stir in corn, cream cheese and instant potato flakes. Heat over low heat until warmed through. Ladle chowder into bowls. Top with cheese, green onions and bacon.
Makes 4 servings

Country Chicken Chowder

Savory Breads

Confetti Scones

   2 teaspoons olive oil
⅓ cup minced red bell pepper
⅓ cup minced green bell pepper
½ teaspoon dried thyme
   1 cup all-purpose flour
¼ cup whole wheat flour
1½ teaspoons baking powder
½ teaspoon baking soda
½ teaspoon sugar
¼ teaspoon ground red pepper
⅛ teaspoon salt
⅓ cup sour cream
⅓ cup milk
¼ cup grated Parmesan cheese
   2 tablespoons minced green onion

1. Preheat oven to 400°F. Line baking sheet with parchment paper; set aside.

2. Heat oil in small skillet over medium heat. Add bell peppers and thyme; cook and stir 5 minutes or until tender.

3. Combine flours, baking powder, baking soda, sugar, ground red pepper and salt in large bowl. Add sour cream, milk, cheese and green onion; mix to form sticky dough. *Do not overmix.*

4. Drop dough by rounded tablespoonfuls onto prepared baking sheet. Place in oven and immediately reduce heat to 375°F. Bake 13 to 15 minutes or until golden. Remove to wire rack; cool completely. *Makes 24 scones*

Wild Rice Three Grain Bread

1 package active dry yeast

⅓ cup warm water (105° to 115°F)

2 cups milk, scalded and cooled to 105° to 115°F

½ cup honey

2 tablespoons butter, melted

2 teaspoons salt

4 to 4½ cups bread flour or unbleached all-purpose flour

2 cups whole wheat flour

½ cup rye flour

½ cup uncooked rolled oats

1 cup cooked wild rice

1 egg, beaten with 1 tablespoon water

½ cup hulled sunflower seeds

In large bowl, dissolve yeast in water. Add milk, honey, butter and salt. Stir in 2 cups bread flour, whole wheat flour, rye flour and oats to make a soft dough. Add wild rice; cover and let rest 15 minutes. Stir in enough additional bread flour to make a stiff dough. Turn dough out onto board and knead 10 minutes. Add more flour as necessary to keep dough from sticking. Turn dough into lightly greased bowl; turn dough over to coat. Cover and let rise until doubled, about 2 hours. Punch down dough. Knead briefly on lightly oiled board. To shape dough, divide into 3 portions; roll into long strands. Braid strands and place on greased baking sheet in wreath shape, or divide in half and place each half in greased 9½×5½-inch loaf pans. Let rise until doubled, about 45 minutes. Brush tops of loaves with egg mixture; slash loaves if desired. Sprinkle with sunflower seeds. Bake at 375°F 45 minutes or until loaves sound hollow when tapped.

Makes 1 braided wreath or 2 loaves

Favorite recipe from **Minnesota Cultivated Wild Rice Council**

Wild Rice Three Grain Bread

Sausage and Cheddar Corn Bread

1 tablespoon vegetable oil
½ pound bulk pork sausage
1 medium onion, diced
1 jalapeño pepper, diced*
1 package (8 ounces) corn muffin mix
1 cup (4 ounces) shredded Cheddar cheese, divided
⅓ cup milk
1 egg

*Jalapeño peppers can sting and irritate the skin, so wear rubber gloves when handling peppers and do not touch your eyes.

1. Heat oil in large cast iron skillet over medium heat. Brown sausage, stirring to break up meat. Add onion and jalapeño; cook and stir 5 minutes or until vegetables are softened. Remove sausage mixture to medium bowl.

2. Preheat oven to 350°F. Combine corn muffin mix, ½ cup cheese, milk and egg in separate medium bowl. Pour batter into skillet. Spread sausage mixture over top. Sprinkle with remaining ½ cup cheese.

3. Bake 20 to 25 minutes or until edges are lightly browned. Cut into wedges. Refrigerate leftovers.   *Makes 10 servings*

Prep Time: 15 minutes
Cook Time: 20 minutes

Popovers

1 cup all-purpose flour
1 cup milk
3 eggs
1 tablespoon butter, softened
½ teaspoon salt

1. Preheat oven to 375°F. Grease and flour 12 standard (2½-inch) muffin cups.

2. Fit processor with steel blade. Add all ingredients to work bowl. Process 2½ minutes continuously.

3. Pour batter into prepared cups, filling each about three-fourths full. Bake 45 to 50 minutes or until dark brown and crispy.   *Makes 12 popovers*

Sausage and Cheddar Corn Bread

Basic White Bread

2 cups warm water (105° to 115°F)
2 packages active dry yeast
2 tablespoons sugar
6 to 6½ cups all-purpose flour, divided
½ cup nonfat dry milk powder
2 tablespoons shortening
2 teaspoons salt

1. Combine water, yeast and sugar in large bowl. Let stand 5 minutes or until bubbly.

2. Add 3 cups flour, milk powder, shortening and salt. Beat with electric mixer at low speed until blended. Increase speed to medium; beat 2 minutes. Stir in enough additional flour, about 3 cups to make soft dough. Turn out onto lightly floured surface. Knead about 10 minutes, adding enough remaining flour to make dough smooth and elastic.

3. Shape dough into ball; place in large greased bowl. Turn dough to grease top. Cover; let rise in warm, draft-free place about 1 hour or until doubled in size.

4. Punch down dough; knead on lightly floured surface 1 minute. Cover with towel; let rest 10 minutes.

5. Grease 2 (8×4-inch) loaf pans; set aside. Divide dough in half. Roll out half of dough into 12×8-inch rectangle with lightly floured rolling pin. Starting with 1 short side, roll up dough jelly-roll style. Pinch seam and ends to seal. Place loaf, seam side down, in prepared pan, tucking ends under. Repeat with remaining dough. Cover; let rise in warm place 1 hour or until doubled in size.

6. Preheat oven to 375°F. Bake 30 to 35 minutes or until loaves are golden brown and sound hollow when tapped. Immediately remove from pans; cool completely on wire racks. *Makes 2 loaves*

Refrigerator White Bread: Prepare and shape dough as directed in steps 1 through 5. Spray 2 sheets of plastic wrap with nonstick cooking spray. Cover dough with plastic wrap, greased side down. Refrigerate 3 to 24 hours. Dough should rise to top of pans during refrigeration. Remove loaves from refrigerator 20 minutes before baking. Preheat oven to 375°F. Remove plastic wrap. Bake 45 to 50 minutes or until loaves are golden brown and sound hollow when tapped. Immediately remove from pans; cool completely on wire racks.

continued on page 32

Basic White Bread

Basic White Bread, continued

Freezer White Bread: Prepare and shape dough as directed in steps 1 through 5. Spray 2 sheets of plastic wrap with nonstick cooking spray. Cover dough with plastic wrap, greased side down. Freeze about 5 hours or until firm. Remove loaves from pans. Wrap frozen loaves securely in plastic wrap; place in labeled plastic freezer bags. Freeze up to 1 month. To bake loaves, unwrap and place in greased loaf pans. Cover with towel; let stand in warm place 4 to 5 hours or until loaves are thawed and doubled in bulk. Preheat oven to 375°F. Bake 40 to 45 minutes or until loaves are golden brown and sound hollow when tapped. Immediately remove from pans; cool completely on wire racks.

Farmer-Style Sour Cream Bread

1 cup sour cream, at room temperature
3 tablespoons water
2½ to 3 cups all-purpose flour, divided
1 package active dry yeast
2 tablespoons sugar
1½ teaspoons salt
¼ teaspoon baking soda
  Vegetable oil
1 tablespoon poppy or sesame seeds

1. Stir together sour cream and water in small saucepan. Heat over low heat until temperature reaches 120° to 130°F. *Do not boil.* Combine 2 cups flour, yeast, sugar, salt and baking soda in large bowl. Stir sour cream mixture into flour mixture until well blended. Turn out dough onto lightly floured surface. Knead about 5 minutes, adding enough remaining flour until dough is smooth and elastic.

2. Grease large baking sheet. Shape dough into ball; place on prepared baking sheet. Flatten into 8-inch circle. Brush top with oil. Sprinkle with poppy seeds. Invert large bowl over dough and let rise in warm place 1 hour or until doubled.

3. Preheat oven to 350°F. Bake 22 to 27 minutes or until golden brown. Remove immediately from baking sheet; cool on wire rack. *Makes 8 to 12 servings*

French Bread

2½ cups warm water (105° to 115°F), divided
2 packages active dry yeast
1 tablespoon sugar
6¾ to 7½ cups bread flour or all-purpose flour, divided
2 teaspoons salt
2 tablespoons yellow cornmeal

1. Combine ½ cup warm water, yeast and sugar in large bowl; let stand 5 minutes or until bubbly. Add 2 cups flour, remaining 2 cups warm water and salt. Beat with electric mixer at low speed until blended. Increase speed to medium; beat 2 minutes. Stir in enough additional flour, about 4¾ cups, to make soft dough.

2. Turn out onto lightly floured surface. Knead about 10 minutes, adding enough remaining flour to make smooth and elastic dough. Shape dough into ball; place in large greased bowl. Turn dough to grease top. Cover with towel; let rise in warm place 1 to 1½ hours or until doubled in bulk.

3. Punch down dough. Knead dough in bowl 1 minute. Cover with towel; let rise in warm place about 1 hour or until doubled in bulk. Grease 2 large baking sheets. Sprinkle with cornmeal; set aside.

4. Punch down dough. Turn out dough onto lightly floured surface; knead several times to remove air bubbles. Cut dough into 4 pieces. Cover with towel; let rest 10 minutes. Roll each piece of dough back and forth, forming loaf about 14 inches long and 2 inches in diameter. Place loaves 4 inches apart on prepared baking sheets. Cut 3 (¼-inch-deep) slashes into each loaf with sharp knife. Brush loaves with water. Cover with towel; let rise in warm place about 35 minutes or until doubled in bulk.

5. Place small baking pan on bottom of oven. Preheat oven to 450°F. Place 2 ice cubes in pan. Brush loaves with water; bake 10 minutes. Rotate baking sheets top to bottom. Quickly spray loaves with cool water using spray mister. Reduce heat to 400°F; bake 10 to 15 minutes more or until loaves are golden brown. Immediately remove from baking sheets; cool on wire racks. Serve warm.

Makes 4 loaves

Onion Buckwheat Bread

1 pound diced white onions
3 tablespoons olive oil
4½ teaspoons yeast
1½ cups water, at 90°F
½ cup milk
6½ cups unbleached bread flour
½ cup buckwheat flour
5 teaspoons sea salt
1 tablespoon finely chopped fresh rosemary
¾ cup (3 ounces) shredded Gouda or Cheddar cheese
Unbleached bread flour as needed for kneading
4 tablespoons poppy seeds or nigella seeds (onion seeds)

1. Sauté onions in olive oil in large skillet over medium-high heat until just browned, about 5 minutes. Set aside to cool.

2. Combine yeast with water in large bowl; let sit 10 minutes until bubbly.

3. Add milk to yeast mixture and stir to combine.

4. Gradually add bread flour, buckwheat flour, salt, rosemary and onions to yeast mixture.

5. When mixture is well combined, add cheese and blend. The dough will be slightly sticky.

6. Knead dough on lightly floured surface about 10 minutes until smooth and elastic. Add additional bread flour as needed if dough is too soft.

7. Lightly oil clean bowl. Place dough in bowl; cover and let rise until doubled in bulk, 1½ to 2 hours.

8. Gently punch down dough and place on lightly floured surface. Cut dough in half and shape into round loaves. Spritz top of each loaf with water and press on poppy seeds or nigella seeds. Place on lightly floured baking sheet; cover and let rise until almost doubled in bulk, 45 minutes to 1 hour.

9. Preheat oven to 450°F. Slash tops of loaves with sharp knife and place in oven. Add steam by placing 2 ice cubes in pan on bottom of oven. Bake 10 minutes. Reduce heat to 400°F and bake an additional 35 to 40 minutes. Cool loaves completely on rack.

Makes 2 (10-inch) round loaves

Favorite recipe from **National Onion Association**

Onion Buckwheat Bread

Freezer Rolls

1¼ cups warm water (100° to 110°F)
  2 envelopes FLEISCHMANN'S® Active Dry Yeast
½ cup sugar
½ cup warm milk (100° to 110°F)
⅓ cup butter or margarine, softened
1½ teaspoons salt
5½ to 6 cups all-purpose flour
  2 large eggs

Place ½ cup warm water in large bowl. Sprinkle yeast over water; stir until dissolved. Add remaining ¾ cup warm water, sugar, warm milk, butter, salt and 2 cups flour. Beat 2 minutes at medium speed of electric mixer. Add eggs and ½ cup flour. Beat at high speed for 2 minutes. Stir in enough remaining flour to make soft dough. Turn out onto lightly floured surface. Knead until smooth and elastic, about 8 to 10 minutes. Cover with plastic wrap; let rest for 20 minutes.

Punch dough down. Shape into desired shapes for dinner rolls. Place on greased baking sheets. Cover with plastic wrap and foil, sealing well. Freeze up to 1 week.*

Once frozen, rolls may be placed in plastic freezer bags.

Remove rolls from freezer; unwrap and place on greased baking sheets. Cover; let rise in warm, draft-free place until doubled in size, about 1½ hours.

Bake at 350°F for 15 minutes or until done. Remove from baking sheets; cool on wire racks.   *Makes about 2 dozen rolls*

*To bake without freezing: After shaping, let rise in warm, draft-free place until doubled in size, about 1 hour. Bake according to above directions.

Shaping the Dough: Crescents: Divide dough in half; roll each half to 14-inch circle. Cut each circle into 12 pie-shaped wedges. Roll up tightly from wide end. Curve ends slightly to form crescents. Knots: Divide dough into 24 equal pieces; roll each into 9-inch rope. Tie once loosely. Coils: Divide dough into 24 equal pieces; roll each into 9-inch rope. Coil each rope and tuck end under the coil. Twists: Divide dough into 24 equal pieces; roll each into 12-inch rope. Fold each rope in half and twist three to four times. Pinch ends to seal.

Freezer Rolls

Roasted Garlic Breadsticks

1 large head garlic*
2 tablespoons olive oil
1 tablespoon water
1 tablespoon butter or margarine, softened
1 cup warm water (110° to 120°F)
1 package active dry yeast
1 teaspoon sugar
2½ to 3 cups all-purpose flour, divided
1 teaspoon salt
1 egg white
1 tablespoon sesame seeds

*Remove outer papery skin from garlic. Place garlic in custard cup. Drizzle with 1 tablespoon oil and 2 tablespoons water. Cover with foil. Bake 1 hour or until garlic cloves are tender. Remove foil and let cool.

1. Preheat oven to 350°F. Break garlic into cloves and finely chop. Combine chopped garlic and butter in small bowl. Cover and set aside.

2. Combine warm water, yeast and sugar in large bowl; let stand 5 minutes or until bubbly. Beat in 1½ cups flour, salt and oil with electric mixer at low speed until blended. Increase speed to medium; beat 2 minutes. Stir in enough additional flour, about 1 cup, with wooden spoon to make soft dough.

3. Turn out onto lightly floured surface. Knead about 5 minutes, adding enough remaining flour until dough is smooth and elastic. Shape dough into ball; place in large greased bowl. Turn dough to grease top. Cover; let rise in warm place about 1 hour or until doubled.

4. Punch down dough; knead on lightly floured surface 1 minute. Cover; let rest 10 minutes. Grease 2 large baking sheets; set aside. Roll dough into 12-inch square with lightly floured rolling pin. Spread garlic mixture evenly over dough. Fold square in half. Roll dough into 14×7-inch rectangle. Cut dough crosswise into 7×1-inch strips.

5. Holding ends of each strip, twist 3 to 4 times. Place strips 2 inches apart on prepared baking sheets, pressing both ends to seal. Cover; let rise in warm place about 30 minutes or until doubled in bulk.

6. Preheat oven to 400°F. Combine egg white and water in small bowl. Brush breadsticks with egg white mixture; sprinkle with sesame seeds. Bake 20 to 22 minutes or until golden. Serve warm.   *Makes 14 breadsticks*

Roasted Garlic Breadsticks

Main Dishes

Roasted Chicken & Vegetables

1 REYNOLDS® Oven Bag, Large Size
1 tablespoon flour
2 cloves garlic, minced
2 tablespoons olive oil
2 tablespoons fresh lemon juice
2 teaspoons dried Italian seasoning
1 whole chicken (3½ to 4 pounds)
2 cups peeled baby carrots, halved lengthwise
1 medium red bell pepper, cut in cubes
1 medium onion, cut in small wedges
   Seasoned salt and black pepper to taste

PREHEAT oven to 350°F.

SHAKE flour in Reynolds Oven Bag; place in 13×9×2-inch or larger baking pan.

ADD garlic, olive oil, lemon juice and Italian seasoning to oven bag. Turn bag to mix with flour. Place chicken in bag. Turn bag to coat chicken with olive oil mixture. Arrange vegetables around chicken. Sprinkle seasoned salt and pepper over chicken and vegetables.

CLOSE oven bag with nylon tie; cut six ½-inch slits in top. Tuck ends of bag in pan.

BAKE 50 to 60 minutes or until meat thermometer reads 180°F.

Makes 4 to 6 servings

Prep Time: 20 minutes
Cook Time: 50 minutes

Peppered Steaks with Caramelized Onions

2 beef shoulder center steaks (Ranch steaks), cut 1 inch thick
   (about 8 ounces each)
2 teaspoons seasoned pepper blend
   Caramelized Onions and Sautéed Spinach (recipe follows)
Roasted Potatoes:
   1 pound unpeeled small red and brown-skinned potatoes, quartered
   1 teaspoon olive oil
   ½ teaspoon dried thyme
   ⅛ teaspoon salt

1. Preheat oven to 425°F. Place potatoes on rimmed baking sheet. Sprinkle with oil, thyme and salt; toss to coat. Roast in oven 30 to 40 minutes or until tender, turning occasionally.

2. Meanwhile, press pepper blend onto beef steaks. Heat large nonstick skillet over medium heat until hot. Place steaks in skillet; cook 13 to 16 minutes for medium rare (145°F) to medium (160°F) doneness, turning twice.

3. Carve steaks; season with salt as desired. Top with onions; serve with potatoes and spinach.   *Makes 4 servings*

Caramelized Onions and Sautéed Spinach: Heat 1 tablespoon butter in large nonstick skillet over medium heat until melted. Add 1 large yellow onion, cut ¼ inch thick; cook 18 to 21 minutes or until caramelized, stirring frequently. Remove onion from skillet; keep warm. Heat 2 teaspoons olive oil and 1 large clove minced garlic over medium heat in same skillet about 30 seconds or until fragrant. Add 8 cups spinach and ⅛ teaspoon salt. Toss to coat and cook 1 minute or until just wilted, stirring frequently. Serve immediately.

Prep and Cook Time: 45 minutes to 1 hour

Favorite recipe from **The Beef Checkoff**

Peppered Steak with Caramelized Onions

Almond-Crusted Salmon with Thyme & Lemon Butter Sauce

¼ **cup plain dry bread crumbs**

¼ **cup blanched almonds**

1 **clove garlic**

2 **tablespoons olive oil**

8 **salmon fillets (about 3 pounds)**

1 **tablespoon cornstarch**

1½ **cups SWANSON® Chicken Stock**

2 **tablespoons lemon juice**

1 **teaspoon chopped fresh thyme leaves** *or*

    ¼ **teaspoon dried thyme leaves, crushed**

3 **tablespoons butter**

¼ **cup chopped shallot or onion**

1. Place the bread crumbs, almonds and garlic into a food processor or blender. Cover and process until the mixture is finely ground. Gradually pour in the olive oil while the food processor is running and process until the mixture is moist.

2. Place the salmon into a roasting pan. Top the salmon with the bread crumb mixture and press to adhere.

3. Bake at 400°F. for 15 minutes or until the salmon flakes easily when tested with a fork and the bread crumb mixture is golden. Remove the salmon from the oven and keep warm.

4. Stir the cornstarch, stock, lemon juice and thyme in a medium bowl until the mixture is smooth.

5. Heat 2 tablespoons butter in a 1-quart saucepan over medium heat. Add the shallots and cook until they're tender. Stir in the cornstarch mixture and heat to a boil. Cook and stir until the sauce boils and thickens. Add the remaining butter and cook and stir until it's melted. Serve the salmon with the sauce.

Makes 8 servings

Prep Time: 15 minutes
Bake Time: 15 minutes

Almond-Crusted Salmon with Thyme & Lemon Butter Sauce

Beef Wellington

1 (2- to 2½-pound) beef tenderloin
Ground black pepper (optional)
½ (17.3-ounce) package PEPPERIDGE FARM® Puff Pastry
    Sheets (1 sheet)
1 egg
1 tablespoon water
1 tablespoon butter
2 cups finely chopped mushrooms
1 medium onion, finely chopped (about ½ cup)

1. Heat the oven to 425°F. Place the beef in a lightly greased roasting pan. Season with the black pepper, if desired. Roast for 30 minutes or until a meat thermometer reads 130°F. Cover the pan and refrigerate for 1 hour.

2. Thaw the pastry sheet at room temperature for 40 minutes or until it's easy to handle. Heat the oven to 425°F. Beat the egg and water in a small bowl with a fork.

3. Heat the butter in a 10-inch skillet over medium-high heat. Add the mushrooms and onion and cook until the vegetables are tender and all the liquid is evaporated, stirring often.

4. Unfold the pastry sheet on a lightly floured surface. Roll the pastry sheet into a rectangle 4 inches longer and 6 inches wider than the beef. Brush the pastry sheet with the egg mixture. Spoon the mushroom mixture onto the pastry sheet to within 1 inch of the edges. Place the beef in the center of the mushroom mixture. Starting at the long sides, fold the pastry over the beef. Place seam-side down on a baking sheet. Tuck the ends under to seal. Brush the pastry with the egg mixture.

5. Bake for 25 minutes or until the pastry is golden and a meat thermometer reads 140°F. Slice and serve warm.   *Makes 10 servings*

Serving Suggestion: Serve with green beans amandine. For dessert, serve with cheesecake topped with sliced strawberries.

Thaw Time: 40 minutes
Prep Time: 30 minutes
Chill Time: 1 hour
Bake Time: 25 minutes

Beef Wellington

Sweet & Spicy Petite Sirloin Steaks with Vegetable Barley "Risotto"

   1 pound boneless beef top sirloin steak, cut ¾ inch thick

   ½ cup ready-to-serve beef broth

   ¼ cup balsamic vinegar

   2 tablespoons jalapeño pepper jelly

    Vegetable Barley "Risotto" (recipe follows)

Seasoning:

   ¾ teaspoon garlic salt

   ¾ teaspoon chili powder

   ½ teaspoon coarse grind black pepper

   ¼ teaspoon ground cumin

   ¼ teaspoon dried oregano leaves

1. Prepare Vegetable Barley "Risotto."

2. Meanwhile, cut beef steak crosswise into four equal "petite" steaks. Combine seasoning ingredients; press evenly into both sides of each steak. Heat large nonstick skillet over medium heat until hot. Place steaks in skillet; cook about 8 to 10 minutes for medium rare (145°F) to medium (160°F) doneness, turning once. Remove steaks; keep warm.

3. Add broth, vinegar and jelly to skillet; cook until browned bits attached to skillet are dissolved and sauce thickens slightly, about 3 to 5 minutes. Spoon sauce over steaks and serve with barley "risotto."   *Makes 4 servings*

Vegetable Barley "Risotto"

   ¾ cup quick-cooking barley

   1 cup coarsely chopped zucchini

   ¼ cup minced shallots

   2 teaspoons olive oil

   1 clove garlic, minced

   1 can (14 to 14½ ounces) ready-to-serve beef broth

   ¾ cup chopped tomatoes

   ¼ teaspoon pepper

continued on page 50

Sweet & Spicy Petite Sirloin Steak with Vegetable Barley "Risotto"

1. Heat large nonstick Dutch oven over medium heat until hot. Add barley and cook, stirring until lightly toasted, about 5 minutes. Add zucchini, shallots, oil and garlic; cook about 3 minutes until zucchini is crisp and tender.

2. Stir in ¾ cup of broth. Bring to a simmer. Cook 5 minutes until liquid is almost absorbed. Add remaining broth; return to simmer and continue cooking 7 to 9 minutes or until barley is tender. Stir in tomatoes and pepper.

Makes 4 servings

Prep and Cook Time: 50 minutes

Favorite recipe from **The Beef Checkoff**

Crusted Tilapia Florentine

> 1 egg
> 2 teaspoons water
> 1 cup Italian-seasoned dry bread crumbs
> 4 fresh tilapia fillets, (about 4 ounces each)
> 2 tablespoons olive oil
> 2⅔ cups PREGO® Traditional Italian Sauce
> 2 cups frozen chopped spinach
> Hot cooked noodles

1. Beat the egg and water with a fork in a shallow dish. Place the bread crumbs on a plate. Dip the fish in the egg mixture, then coat with the bread crumbs.

2. Heat the oil in a 12-inch skillet over medium-high heat. Add the fish and cook for 8 minutes, turning once or until the fish flakes easily when tested with a fork. Remove the fish and keep warm.

3. Stir the sauce and spinach into the skillet. Heat to a boil. Reduce the heat to medium. Cook for 2 minutes or until the spinach is wilted. Serve the sauce over the fish. Serve with the noodles.

Makes 4 servings

Prep Time: 10 minutes
Cook Time: 15 minutes

Roasted Turkey Breast
with Herbed Au Jus

1 tablespoon all-purpose flour
1 plastic oven bag, turkey size
1 cup SWANSON® Chicken Stock
½ teaspoon *each* ground dried sage leaves, dried rosemary
     and thyme leaves, crushed
1 (6- to 8-pound) bone-in turkey breast
½ teaspoon paprika (optional)
1 can (10½ ounce) CAMPBELL'S® Turkey Gravy

1. Add the flour to the oven bag. Close and shake the bag to distribute the flour. Place the bag in a 13×9×2-inch baking pan. Add the stock, sage, rosemary and thyme to the bag. Squeeze the bag to blend in the flour.

2. Rinse the turkey with cold water and pat dry with a paper towel. Sprinkle the turkey evenly with the paprika. Add the turkey to the bag. Close the bag with the nylon tie. Cut 6 (½-inch) slits in the top of the bag. Insert a meat thermometer through a slit in the bag into the thickest part of the meat, making sure the thermometer is not touching the bone.

3. Roast the turkey at 350°F. for 1¾ to 2 hours.* Begin checking for doneness after 1½ hours of roasting time. Let the turkey stand for 10 minutes before slicing.

4. Remove the turkey from the bag. Pour the turkey liquid from the bag into a large cup. Skim off the fat.

5. Heat the turkey liquid and gravy in a 2-quart saucepan over medium heat until hot. Serve with the turkey.   *Makes 6 servings*

The internal temperature of the turkey should reach 170°F.

Prep Time: 10 minutes
Cook Time: 2 hours
Stand Time: 10 minutes

Southern Fried Catfish with Hush Puppies

Hush Puppy Batter (recipe follows)
4 catfish fillets (about 1½ pounds)
½ cup yellow cornmeal
3 tablespoons all-purpose flour
1½ teaspoons salt
¼ teaspoon ground red pepper
Vegetable oil

1. Prepare Hush Puppy Batter; set aside.

2. Rinse catfish; pat dry with paper towels. Combine cornmeal, flour, salt and red pepper in shallow dish. Dip fish into cornmeal mixture. Heat 1 inch oil in large heavy skillet over medium heat until 375°F on deep-fry thermometer.

3. Cook fish in batches 4 to 5 minutes or until golden brown and fish begins to flake when tested with fork. Allow temperature of oil to return to 375°F between batches. Drain fish on paper towels.

4. To make Hush Puppies, drop batter by tablespoonfuls into hot oil. Cook in batches 2 minutes or until golden brown. Drain on paper towels.

Makes 4 servings

Hush Puppy Batter

1½ cups yellow cornmeal
½ cup all-purpose flour
2 teaspoons baking powder
½ teaspoon salt
1 cup milk
1 small onion, minced
1 egg, lightly beaten

1. Combine cornmeal, flour, baking powder and salt in medium bowl. Add milk, onion and egg. Stir until well blended.

2. Allow batter to stand 5 to 10 minutes before frying.

Makes about 24 hush puppies

Southern Fried Catfish with Hush Puppies

Cherry & Mushroom Stuffed Pork Chops

- 2 tablespoons vegetable oil, divided
- 1 cup chopped fresh shiitake mushrooms
- ¼ cup finely chopped onion
- ¼ cup finely chopped celery
- ¼ cup dried sweetened cherries, chopped
- ¼ teaspoon salt
- ⅛ teaspoon dried thyme
- ⅛ teaspoon black pepper
- 4 boneless pork loin chops (about 1¼ pounds), cut 1 inch thick
- 1 teaspoon all-purpose flour
- ¼ cup chicken broth
- ¼ cup cherry juice

1. Heat 1 tablespoon oil in 12-inch skillet. Add mushrooms, onion and celery; cook and stir over medium-high heat 4 minutes. Stir in cherries, salt, thyme and pepper. Remove from heat.

2. Make deep pocket in side of each pork chop; fill with one fourth of cherry stuffing. Skewer pockets closed with toothpicks.

3. Heat remaining 1 tablespoon oil in same skillet over medium heat. Add pork chops. Brown over medium heat 7 to 8 minutes per side or until cooked through.

4. Remove pork from skillet. Pour off fat. Add flour to skillet; cook 30 seconds, stirring constantly. Stir in broth and juice, scraping up browned bits from bottom of skillet. Cook 1 minute to thicken sauce slightly.

5. Return pork chops to skillet and turn to coat evenly. Spoon sauce over pork to serve.

Makes 4 servings

Cherry & Mushroom Stuffed Pork Chop

Pesto Meatballs with Spaghetti

  1 pound ground turkey
  ⅓ cup plain dry bread crumbs
  ¼ cup grated Parmesan cheese
  ¼ cup milk
  2 teaspoons dried basil
  ½ teaspoon garlic powder
  ½ teaspoon black pepper
  1 tablespoon olive oil
  1 can (about 14 ounces) stewed tomatoes
1½ cups chopped mushrooms
  1 medium green bell pepper, seeded and chopped
  ½ cup chopped onions
  6 cups hot cooked spaghetti

1. Combine turkey, bread crumbs, cheese, milk, basil, garlic powder and black pepper in large bowl; mix well. Shape into 24 meatballs.

2. Heat oil in nonstick skillet over medium-high heat. Add tomatoes, mushrooms, bell pepper and onions; simmer 5 to 6 minutes or until softened. Add meatballs to skillet in 2 batches; cook 5 to 6 minutes or until lightly browned on all sides. Cook additional 10 to 15 minutes or until cooked through.

3. Serve meatballs and sauce over spaghetti.   *Makes 6 servings*

To quickly shape uniform meatballs, place the turkey mixture on a cutting board and pat evenly into large square, one inch thick. With sharp knife, cut into 1-inch squares and shape each into a ball.

Pesto Meatballs with Spaghetti

On the Side

Macaroni and Cheese with Mixed Vegetables

1¼ cups milk, divided

  2 tablespoons all-purpose flour

½ cup shredded sharp Cheddar cheese

½ cup shredded Parmesan cheese

1½ cups frozen mixed vegetables, cooked and drained

1⅓ cups cooked whole wheat elbow macaroni, rotini or penne

¼ teaspoon salt (optional)

⅛ teaspoon black pepper

1. Preheat oven to 325°F. Coat 1½-quart glass baking dish with nonstick cooking spray; set aside.

2. Combine ¼ cup milk and flour in small bowl until smooth. Add remaining milk; stir until well blended. Pour into small saucepan. Bring mixture to a simmer over medium heat, stirring constantly, until thickened.

3. Combine cheeses in separate medium bowl. Stir half of cheese mixture into saucepan. Reserve remaining cheese mixture. Add vegetables, macaroni, salt, if desired, and pepper to saucepan.

4. Spoon macaroni mixture into prepared baking dish. Sprinkle with reserved cheese. Bake 20 minutes or until cheese melts and macaroni is heated through. Remove from oven. Let stand 5 minutes before serving.   *Makes 4 servings*

Corny Corn Fritters

2 cups vegetable oil
1 package (12 count) ORTEGA® Taco Shells
¾ cup all-purpose flour
2 teaspoons baking powder
½ teaspoon baking soda
2 eggs
1 cup milk
1 cup frozen whole-kernel corn, thawed
ORTEGA® Black Bean & Corn Salsa

Heat oil in medium saucepan over medium-high heat to 375°F. Line platter with paper towels.

Place taco shells in resealable plastic bag; close bag. Crush with rolling pin until finely ground. Place crumbs in medium bowl. Add flour, baking powder and baking soda; mix well.

Combine eggs and milk in small bowl; mix well. Pour egg mixture into dry ingredients; mix well. Fold in corn. Let stand 10 minutes.

Place heaping tablespoonfuls of mixture into hot oil. Cook 4 minutes or until golden brown. Remove with slotted spoon. Drain on paper towels. Serve with salsa for dipping.   *Makes about 30 fritters*

Tip: For cheesy corn fritters, add 1 cup finely shredded Cheddar cheese to the fritter mixture along with the egg mixture.

Prep Time: 15 minutes
Start to Finish: 20 minutes

Corny Corn Fritters

Cheesy Green Bean Casserole

¾ **cup milk**
2 **teaspoons all-purpose flour**
1 **teaspoon dried minced onion**
½ **teaspoon black pepper**
1 **package (16 ounces) frozen cut green beans, thawed**
1 **cup (4 ounces) shredded Cheddar cheese, divided**
¼ **cup seasoned dry bread crumbs**

1. Preheat oven to 350°F.

2. Whisk milk, flour, dried onion and pepper in 1½-quart baking dish until well blended. Stir in green beans and ½ cup cheese.

3. Bake, uncovered, 25 minutes. Sprinkle with remaining ½ cup cheese and bread crumbs. Bake 5 minutes or until cheese is melted.   *Makes 6 servings*

Potatoes au Gratin

4 to 6 **medium unpeeled baking potatoes (about 2 pounds)**
2 **cups (8 ounces) shredded Cheddar cheese**
1 **cup (4 ounces) shredded Swiss cheese**
2 **tablespoons butter**
3 **tablespoons all-purpose flour**
2½ **cups milk**
2 **tablespoons Dijon mustard**
¼ **teaspoon salt**
¼ **teaspoon black pepper**

1. Preheat oven to 400°F. Grease 13×9-inch baking dish.

2. Cut potatoes into thin slices. Layer potatoes in prepared dish. Top with cheeses.

3. Melt butter in medium saucepan over medium heat. Stir in flour; cook 1 minute. Stir in milk, mustard, salt and pepper; bring to a boil. Reduce heat; cook, stirring constantly, until mixture thickens. Pour milk mixture over cheese. Cover pan with foil.

4. Bake 30 minutes. Remove foil; bake 15 to 20 minutes or until potatoes are tender and top is browned. Let stand 10 minutes before serving.

Makes 6 to 8 servings

Cheesy Green Bean Casserole

Cran-Orange Acorn Squash

3 small acorn squash

5 tablespoons instant brown rice

3 tablespoons minced onion

3 tablespoons diced celery

3 tablespoons dried cranberries

   Pinch ground or dried sage

1 teaspoon butter, cut into bits

3 tablespoons orange juice

½ cup warm water

Slow Cooker Directions

1. Slice off tops of squash and enough of bottoms so squash will sit upright. Scoop out seeds and discard; set squash aside.

2. Combine rice, onion, celery, cranberries and sage in small bowl. Stuff each squash with rice mixture; dot with butter. Pour 1 tablespoon orange juice into each squash over stuffing. Stand squash in slow cooker. Pour water into bottom of slow cooker.

3. Cover; cook on LOW 2½ hours or until squash are tender.

Makes 6 servings

Prep Time: 20 minutes
Cook Time: 2½ hours (LOW)

---

*The skin of squash can defy
even the sharpest knives.
To make slicing easier,
microwave the whole squash
at HIGH 5 minutes
to soften the skin.*

Cran-Orange Acorn Squash

Chive & Onion Mashed Potatoes

    2 pounds potatoes, peeled, quartered (about 6 cups)
 ½ cup milk
    1 tub (8 ounces) PHILADELPHIA® Chive & Onion
        Cream Cheese Spread
 ¼ cup KRAFT® Ranch Dressing

1. Place potatoes and enough water to cover in 3-quart saucepan. Bring to a boil.

2. Reduce heat to medium; cook 20 to 25 minutes or until tender. Drain.

3. Mash potatoes, gradually stirring in milk, cream cheese spread and dressing until light and fluffy. Serve immediately.   *Makes 10 servings, ½ cup each*

Make Ahead: Mix ingredients as directed; spoon into 1½-quart casserole dish. Cover. Refrigerate several hours or overnight. When ready to serve, bake, uncovered, at 350°F 1 hour or until heated through.

Prep Time: 10 minutes
Cook Time: 25 minutes

Savory Matchstick Carrots

 ½ pound carrots, cut into julienne strips
    1 small turnip, cut into julienne strips*
 ½ cup water
    3 tablespoons butter or margarine, cut into chunks
 1½ teaspoons fresh thyme *or* ½ teaspoon dried thyme
        Salt and black pepper

*Or substitute two additional carrots for turnip.

1. Place carrot and turnip strips in medium saucepan. Add water; cover. Bring to a boil over high heat; reduce heat to medium. Simmer 5 to 8 minutes or until crisp-tender.

2. Drain vegetables in colander. Melt butter over medium heat in same saucepan; stir in thyme, salt and pepper. Add carrots; toss gently to coat.

Makes 4 servings

Chive & Onion Mashed Potatoes

Harvest Fruit Stuffing

1¾ cups SWANSON® Chicken Broth (Regular, Natural
    Goodness™ or Certified Organic)
¼ cup apple juice
1 cup cut-up mixed dried fruit
1 stalk celery, sliced (about ½ cup)
1 medium onion chopped (about ½ cup)
5 cups PEPPERIDGE FARM® Herb Seasoned Stuffing

1. Stir the broth, apple juice, dried fruit, celery and onion in a large saucepan.
Heat to a boil over medium-high heat. Reduce the heat to low. Cover and cook
5 minutes or until the vegetables are tender. Remove from the heat. Add the
stuffing and stir lightly to coat.

2. Spoon into a 1½-quart casserole. Bake at 350°F. for 20 minutes or until hot.

Makes 8 servings

Prep Time: 20 minutes
Cook Time: 10 minutes
Bake Time: 20 minutes

Garlicky Mustard Greens

2 pounds mustard greens
1 teaspoon olive oil
1 cup chopped onion
2 cloves garlic, minced
¾ cup chopped red bell pepper
½ cup chicken broth*
1 tablespoon cider vinegar
1 teaspoon sugar

1. Remove stems and any wilted leaves from greens. Stack several leaves; roll up
jelly-roll style. Cut crosswise into 1-inch slices. Repeat with remaining greens.

2. Heat oil in large saucepan over medium heat. Add onion and garlic; cook
and stir 5 minutes or until onion is tender. Stir in greens, bell pepper and broth.
Reduce heat to low. Cook, covered, 25 minutes or until greens are tender, stirring
occasionally.

3. Combine vinegar and sugar in small cup; stir until sugar is dissolved. Stir into
cooked greens; remove from heat. Serve immediately.   *Makes 4 servings*

Harvest Fruit Stuffing

Pumpkin Apple Mash

2 tablespoons butter

1 small onion, chopped (about ¼ cup)

¾ cup SWANSON® Chicken Broth (Regular, Natural Goodness™ or Certified Organic)

1 tablespoon packed brown sugar

¼ teaspoon dried thyme leaves, crushed

⅛ teaspoon ground black pepper

1 pumpkin or calabaza squash (about 2½ pounds), peeled, seeded and cut into 1-inch pieces (about 5 to 6 cups)

2 medium Macintosh apples, peeled, cored and cut into 1-inch pieces

1. Heat the butter in a 4-quart saucepan over medium-high heat. Add the onion and cook until the onion is tender-crisp.

2. Add the broth, brown sugar, thyme, black pepper and pumpkin and heat the mixture to a boil. Cover and reduce the heat to low. Cook for 10 minutes or until the vegetables are tender.

3. Add the apples. Cook for 5 minutes more or until the apples are tender.

4. Mash the vegetable mixture with a fork or potato masher. Serve immediately.

Makes 4 servings

Prep Time: 10 minutes
Cook Time: 20 minutes

Cob Corn in Barbecue Butter

4 ears fresh corn, shucked

2 tablespoons butter, softened

½ teaspoon dry barbecue seasoning

¼ teaspoon salt

1. Pour 1 inch of water into large saucepan. Bring to a boil over medium-high heat. Add corn; cover. Cook 4 to 6 minutes or until kernels are slightly crisp when pierced with fork.

2. Blend butter, barbecue seasoning and salt in small bowl until smooth. Serve with corn.

Makes 4 servings

Pumpkin Apple Mash

Greens 'n' Taters

2 cups beet greens

4 medium potatoes, peeled and cut into 1-inch cubes

Nonstick cooking spray

¼ cup chopped onion

1 clove garlic, minced

½ teaspoon whole fennel seeds, crushed

¼ cup plain yogurt

3 to 4 tablespoons warm milk

1 tablespoon butter

½ teaspoon salt

¼ teaspoon black pepper

1. Wash beet greens. Drain but do not pat dry; leave some water clinging to leaves. Remove stems; thinly slice. Set aside.

2. Place potatoes and 1 inch of water in medium saucepan. Bring to a boil over high heat. Reduce heat to medium-low. Simmer, covered, 10 to 12 minutes or until potatoes are fork-tender. Drain; set aside.

3. Coat small skillet with cooking spray. Add onion, garlic and fennel seeds; cook and stir over medium heat about 5 minutes or until onion is softened. Add beet greens; cook 5 to 7 minutes or until greens are wilted and tender.

4. Mash potatoes with potato masher or beat with electric mixer; beat in yogurt, milk, butter, salt and pepper. Stir in beet green mixture. Serve immediately.

Makes 6 servings

Beet tops are frequently bunched together and sold separately as beet greens. They should be fresh looking and dark green, not wilted or slimy.

Greens 'n' Taters

Sweet Endings

Deep-Dish Country Apple Pie

5 cups sliced Gala apples

3 cups sliced Granny Smith apples

1 tablespoon lemon juice

2 teaspoons vanilla

¼ cup all-purpose flour

½ cup sugar

½ teaspoon ground cinnamon

¼ teaspoon ground nutmeg

2 tablespoons butter or margarine

1 prepared refrigerated pie crust

1. Preheat oven to 425°F. Combine apples, lemon juice and vanilla in large bowl; toss to coat. Add flour, sugar, cinnamon and nutmeg; toss again. Transfer to 9-inch deep-dish pie pan. Dot with butter.

2. Cover with crust. Cut several slits in crust. Bake 50 minutes or until apples are tender. (Cover edges with foil during last 15 minutes if browning too quickly.)

3. Serve warm or at room temperature. Store leftovers, covered, in refrigerator.

Makes 8 servings

Upside-Down Peach Corn Bread Cakes

   4 tablespoons butter, divided
 $\frac{1}{2}$ cup packed light brown sugar, divided
   1 fresh peach, thinly sliced
   2 packages ($8\frac{1}{2}$ ounces) corn bread mix
   2 eggs
 $\frac{1}{2}$ cup milk
   2 tablespoons vegetable oil
 $1\frac{3}{4}$ cups diced fresh peaches

1. Preheat oven to 400°F. Spray 8 standard ($2\frac{1}{2}$-inch) muffin cups with nonstick cooking spray. Place $1\frac{1}{2}$ teaspoons butter and 1 tablespoon brown sugar in bottom of each ramekin. Divide peach slices equally among ramekins.

2. Whisk together corn bread mix, eggs, milk and oil in large bowl. Stir in diced peaches. Pour $\frac{3}{4}$ cup batter into each muffin cup. Bake 20 minutes or until golden and toothpick inserted into centers comes out clean. Let cool 5 minutes. Run knife around edges. Invert cakes onto serving plates.   *Makes 8 servings*

Red Velvet Cake

   1 package (2-layer size) white cake mix
   2 squares BAKER'S® Unsweetened Baking Chocolate, melted
   1 tablespoon red food coloring
   1 package (8 ounces) PHILADELPHIA® Cream Cheese, softened
 $\frac{1}{2}$ cup (1 stick) butter or margarine, melted
   1 package (16 ounces) powdered sugar (about 4 cups)
 $\frac{1}{2}$ cup chopped PLANTERS® Pecans

1. Prepare and bake cake mix as directed on package for 2 (9-inch) round cake layers, adding chocolate and food coloring with water, eggs and oil; cool completely.

2. Beat cream cheese and butter with electric mixer on medium speed until well blended. Gradually add sugar, beating well after each addition. Stir in pecans.

3. Fill and frost cake layers with cream cheese frosting.   *Makes 16 servings*

Prep Time: 10 minutes
Bake Time: as directed

Upside-Down Peach Corn Bread Cakes

Cherry Almond Blonde Brownies

REYNOLDS® Parchment Paper

1 cup flour

1 teaspoon baking powder

¼ teaspoon salt

¾ cup packed light brown sugar

½ cup (1 stick) butter, softened

2 eggs

⅓ cup milk

1 teaspoon vanilla

1 teaspoon almond extract

¾ cup sliced almonds, coarsely chopped, divided

½ cup sweetened dried cherries

½ cup white chocolate chips

PREHEAT oven to 350°F. Line a 13×9×2-inch baking pan with Reynolds Parchment Paper, creasing folds into corners to fit pan, extending paper up sides of pan; set aside.

COMBINE flour, baking powder and salt on a sheet of parchment paper; set aside.

BEAT together brown sugar and butter in a large bowl on medium speed of an electric mixer until light and fluffy. Add eggs, milk, vanilla and almond extracts; beat well. Beat in flour mixture until well blended. Stir in ½ cup almonds, cherries and white chocolate chips.

SPREAD dough evenly in parchment-lined pan. Sprinkle remaining ¼ cup almonds on top.

BAKE 25 to 27 minutes. Cool in pan on wire rack. Use edges of parchment to lift brownies from pan onto a cutting board. Pull back edges of parchment for easy cutting. Cut into bars. *Makes 24 servings*

Prep Time: 10 minutes
Cook Time: 25 minutes

Cherry Almond Blonde Brownies

Perfect Pumpkin Pie

1 (15-ounce) can pumpkin (about 2 cups)
1 (14-ounce) can EAGLE BRAND® Sweetened Condensed Milk
   (NOT evaporated milk)
2 eggs
1 teaspoon ground cinnamon
½ teaspoon ground ginger
½ teaspoon ground nutmeg
½ teaspoon salt
1 (9-inch) unbaked pie crust

1. Preheat oven to 425°F.

2. In medium bowl, whisk pumpkin, EAGLE BRAND®, eggs, cinnamon, ginger, nutmeg and salt until smooth. Pour into crust.

3. Bake 15 minutes. Reduce oven temperature to 350°F and continue baking 35 to 40 minutes longer or until knife inserted 1 inch from crust comes out clean. Cool. Garnish as desired. Store leftovers covered in refrigerator.

Makes one (9-inch) pie

Sour Cream Topping: In medium bowl, combine 1½ cups sour cream, 2 tablespoons granulated sugar and 1 teaspoon vanilla extract. After pie has baked 30 minutes at 350°F, spread mixture evenly over top; bake 10 minutes longer.

Streusel Topping: In medium bowl, combine ½ cup packed brown sugar and ½ cup all-purpose flour; cut in ¼ cup (½ stick) cold butter or margarine until crumbly. Stir in ¼ cup chopped nuts. After pie has baked 30 minutes at 350°F, sprinkle streusel evenly over top; bake 10 minutes longer.

Chocolate Glaze: In small saucepan over low heat, melt ½ cup semisweet chocolate chips and 1 teaspoon solid shortening. Drizzle or spread over top of baked pie.

Prep Time: 15 minutes
Bake Time: 50 to 55 minutes

Perfect Pumpkin Pie

Best Fudgey Pecan Brownies

½ cup (1 stick) butter or margarine, melted
1 cup sugar
1 teaspoon vanilla extract
2 eggs
½ cup all-purpose flour
⅓ cup HERSHEY'S Cocoa
¼ teaspoon baking powder
¼ teaspoon salt
½ cup coarsely chopped pecans
Chocolate Pecan Frosting (recipe follows)
Pecan halves

1. Heat oven to 350°F. Lightly grease 8- or 9-inch square baking pan.

2. Beat butter, sugar and vanilla with spoon in large bowl. Add eggs; beat well. Stir together flour, cocoa, baking powder and salt; gradually add to egg mixture, beating until well blended. Stir in chopped pecans. Spread in prepared pan.

3. Bake 20 to 25 minutes or until brownies begin to pull away from sides of pan. Meanwhile, prepare Chocolate Pecan Frosting. Spread warm frosting over warm brownies. Garnish with pecan halves. Cool completely; cut into squares.

Makes about 16 brownies

Chocolate Pecan Frosting

1⅓ cups powdered sugar
2 tablespoons HERSHEY'S Cocoa
3 tablespoons butter or margarine
2 tablespoons milk
¼ teaspoon vanilla extract
¼ cup chopped pecans

1. Place powdered sugar and cocoa in medium bowl.

2. Heat butter and milk in small saucepan over low heat until butter is melted. Gradually beat into cocoa mixture, beating until smooth. Stir in vanilla and pecans.

Makes about 1 cup

Best Fudgey Pecan Brownies

Strawberry-Swirl Cake

1 package (2-layer size) white cake mix
1 package (4-serving size) JELL-O® Strawberry Flavor Gelatin
⅔ cup BREAKSTONE'S® or KNUDSEN® Sour Cream
⅔ cup powdered sugar
1 tub (8 ounces) COOL WHIP® Whipped Topping, thawed
1 cup sliced strawberries, plus 2 whole strawberries for garnish

PREHEAT oven to 350°F. Grease 2 (8- or 9-inch) round cake pans; set aside. Prepare cake batter as directed on package. Pour half of the batter into medium bowl. Add dry gelatin mix; stir until well blended. Spoon half of the white batter and half of the pink batter, side by side, into each prepared pan. Lightly swirl batters together using a teaspoon. (Do not overswirl, or the color of the cake will be all pink and not pink and white marbled.)

BAKE 30 minutes. Cool 30 minutes in pans. Remove to wire racks; cool completely.

MIX sour cream and powdered sugar in medium bowl until well blended. Gently stir in whipped topping. Place 1 of the cake layers on serving plate; spread top with 1 cup of the whipped topping mixture. Top with 1 cup of the strawberries and remaining cake layer. Spread top and sides of cake with remaining whipped topping mixture. Garnish with whole strawberries just before serving. Store leftover cake in refrigerator. *Makes 16 servings, 1 slice each*

How to Prevent Air Bubbles: To release any air bubbles from the cake batter, lightly tap cake pans on counter before baking. Any small air bubbles will rise to the surface.

Prep Time: 35 minutes
Total Time: 1 hour 35 minutes (includes cooling)

Strawberry-Swirl Cake

Apple Pecan Cheesecake

1½ cups HONEY MAID® Graham Cracker Crumbs

¼ cup (½ stick) butter, melted

2 tablespoons firmly packed brown sugar

4 packages (8 ounces each) PHILADELPHIA® Cream Cheese, softened

1½ cups firmly packed brown sugar, divided

1 teaspoon vanilla

1 cup BREAKSTONE'S® or KNUDSEN® Sour Cream

4 eggs

4 cups chopped peeled apples (about 3 medium)

¾ cup PLANTERS® Chopped Pecans

1 teaspoon ground cinnamon

1. Preheat oven to 325°F. Line 13×9-inch baking pan with foil, with ends of foil extending over sides of pan. Mix crumbs, butter and 2 tablespoons brown sugar; press firmly onto bottom of pan.

2. Beat cream cheese, 1 cup of the brown sugar and the vanilla in large bowl with electric mixer on medium speed until well blended. Add sour cream; mix well. Add eggs, 1 at a time, mixing on low speed after each addition just until blended. Pour over crust. Mix remaining ½ cup brown sugar, the apples, pecans and cinnamon; spoon evenly over cheesecake batter.

3. Bake 55 minutes or until center is almost set. Cool. Refrigerate 4 hours or overnight. Let stand at room temperature 30 minutes before serving. Lift cheesecake from pan using foil handles. Cut into 16 pieces. Store leftover cheesecake in refrigerator.   *Makes 16 servings, 1 piece each*

Jazz it Up: For an extra special touch, drizzle KRAFT® Caramel Topping over each piece of cheesecake just before serving.

Best of Season: Take advantage of the many varieties of apples that are available. Try using Jonathan, Granny Smith or Honeycrisp for the topping.

Prep Time: 15 minutes plus refrigerating
Bake Time: 55 minutes

Apple Pecan Cheesecake

Chocolate-Raspberry Torte

1 package (8 ounce) BAKER'S® Semi-Sweet Baking Chocolate, divided
1 package (2-layer size) devil's food cake mix
1 package (8 ounces) PHILADELPHIA® Cream Cheese, softened
4 squares BAKER'S® Premium White Baking Chocolate, melted, cooled
1 tub (8 ounces) COOL WHIP® Whipped Topping, thawed, divided
1 cup seedless raspberry jam
1 cup raspberries

1. Melt 4 of the semi-sweet chocolate squares as directed on package; cool slightly. Prepare cake batter as directed on package, adding the melted semi-sweet chocolate with the water; pour into prepared 2 (9-inch) round baking pans. Bake as directed on package. Cool in pan 10 minutes; remove to wire rack. Cool completely. Wrap cake layers tightly in plastic wrap; freeze 1 hour.

2. Meanwhile, beat cream cheese in large bowl with electric mixer until creamy. Add melted white chocolate; mix well. Gently stir in half of the whipped topping. Refrigerate until ready to use.

3. Cut each cake layer horizontally in half. (You will have 4 layers.) Place 1 of the bottom cake layers on serving plate; spread top with $\frac{1}{3}$ cup of the jam. Top with $\frac{2}{3}$ cup of the cream cheese mixture. Repeat cake, jam and cream cheese mixture layers 2 more times; top with remaining cake layer.

4. Microwave remaining whipped topping and remaining 4 semi-sweet chocolate squares in microwaveable bowl on HIGH 1 minute; stir. Microwave an additional 30 seconds or until chocolate is melted. Stir until well blended. Spread over top of torte. Garnish with raspberries. Store in refrigerator. *Makes 18 servings*

Jazz it Up: Garnish with chocolate curls made from additional chocolate squares.

Prep Time: 25 minutes

Chocolate-Raspberry Torte

Extra Chunky Peanut Butter Cookies

2 cups all-purpose flour
1 teaspoon baking soda
½ teaspoon salt
1 cup chunky peanut butter
¾ cup granulated sugar
½ cup packed light brown sugar
½ cup (1 stick) butter, softened
2 eggs
1 teaspoon vanilla
1½ cups chopped chocolate-covered peanut butter cups
     (12 to 14 candies)
1 cup dry roasted peanuts

1. Preheat oven to 350°F. Line cookie sheets with parchment paper or lightly grease.

2. Combine flour, baking soda and salt in medium bowl. Beat peanut butter, granulated sugar, brown sugar and butter in large bowl with electric mixer at medium speed until creamy. Beat in eggs and vanilla. Add flour mixture; beat until well blended. Stir in chopped candy and peanuts. Drop dough by rounded tablespoonfuls 2 inches apart on prepared cookie sheets.

3. Bake 13 minutes or until set. Cool on cookie sheets 1 minute. Remove to wire racks; cool completely.   *Makes about 4 dozen cookies*

Cookies that are uniform in size and shape will finish baking at the same time. To easily shape drop cookies into a uniform size, use an ice cream scoop with a release bar.

Extra Chunky Peanut Butter Cookies

Acknowledgments

The publisher would like to thank the companies and organizations listed below for the use of their recipes and photographs in this publication.

ACH Food Companies, Inc.

Courtesy The Beef Checkoff

Campbell Soup Company

ConAgra Foods, Inc.

EAGLE BRAND®

The Hershey Company

Hormel Foods, LLC

Idaho Potato Commission

©2010 Kraft Foods, KRAFT, KRAFT Hexagon Logo, PHILADELPHIA AND PHILADELPHIA Logo are registered trademarks of Kraft Foods Holdings, Inc. All rights reserved.

Minnesota Cultivated Wild Rice Council

National Onion Association

Newman's Own, Inc.®

North Dakota Wheat Commission

Ortega®, A Division of B&G Foods, Inc.

Reckitt Benckiser Inc.

Recipes courtesy of the Reynolds Kitchens

Tyson Foods, Inc.